ISO/IEC 27701:2025

An introduction to privacy information management systems

ISO/IEC 27701:2025

An introduction to privacy information management systems

ALAN SHIPMAN AND STEVE WATKINS

GRC Solutions

GRC Solutions
Unit 3, Clive Court
Bartholomew's Walk
Cambridgeshire Business Park
Ely, Cambridgeshire
CB7 4EA
United Kingdom
www.itgovernance.co.uk

First published in the United Kingdom in 2025 by GRC Solutions
ISBN: 978-1-78778-608-0

ABOUT THE AUTHORS

Alan Shipman: Managing Director, Group 5 Training Limited.

Alan acted as project editor for the world's first privacy information management international standard (ISO/IEC 27701:2019).

He is Chair of IST/33/5, which is responsible for the UK's contributions to the work of ISO/IEC JTC1/SC27/WG5, which deals with identity management and privacy technologies.

Alan has more than 30 years' experience managing personal information, both as a data processor for a service organisation and as a data controller. He is a regular speaker at conferences, covering all aspects of information management. Alan has been involved in the development of BS 10008 throughout its life (first published as guidance in 1996). This deals with the management of electronic information of all types, including the conversion of paper-based information to electronic forms. His experience includes advising organisations in both the public and private sector on the implementation of BS 10008.

Alan can be contacted at *a.shipman@group5.co.uk*.

Steve Watkins is a director at Kinsnall Consulting Ltd. He is a contracted technical assessor for UKAS – advising on its assessments of certification bodies offering ISO/IEC 27701/PIMS, ISO/IEC 27001/ISMS and ISO/IEC 20000-1/ITSMS accredited certification, and undertakes information security assessments of forensic science laboratories seeking accreditation to the Forensic Science Regulator's codes of practice and conduct.

Steve is a member of ISO/IEC JTC 1/SC 27, the international technical committee responsible for information security, cyber security and privacy standards, and from 2018 to 2025 chaired the UK National Standards Body's technical committee IST/33 (information security, cyber security and privacy protection) that mirrors it. He is the ISO representative on the EU/ENISA Stakeholder Cybersecurity Certification Group (SCCG).

Steve can be contacted at *SteveGWatkins@Kinsnall.com*.

CONTENTS

INTRODUCTION

This pocket guide has been updated to align with the 2025 edition of ISO/IEC 27701, reflecting the separation of the privacy information management system (PIMS) standard from the information security management system standard (ISO/IEC 27001) that the previous version of the PIMS standard extended.

The guide provides a concise introduction to such considerations, aiding those organisations looking to improve their privacy information management regime, particularly where ISO/IEC 27701:2025 is involved.

It is intended for:

- People looking for general information about a PIMS; and
- Organisations implementing, or considering improving, their PIMS, particularly where ISO/IEC 27701:2025 is being considered.

It will enable you to understand the basics of privacy information management, including:

- What privacy information management means;
- How to manage privacy information successfully using a PIMS aligned to ISO/IEC 27701;
- Key areas of investment for a business-focused PIMS; and
- How your organisation can demonstrate the degree of assurance it offers with regard to privacy information management.

This guide will prove useful at a number of stages in any privacy information management project, including:

- At the decision-making stage, to ensure that those committing to a privacy information management project do so from an informed position;
- At project initiation, as an introduction to privacy information management for the project board, project

team members and those on the periphery of the project; and

- As part of an ongoing awareness campaign, being made available to all staff and to new starters as part of their induction.

A word of warning: this is not an implementation or 'How to' guide.

Implementing an ISO/IEC 27701-conforming PIMS requires more advice than can be covered in a pocket guide. A project of this nature is, in most cases, likely to equate to a significant business-change project, and will require all the project governance arrangements that suit such an undertaking.

CHAPTER 1: WHAT IS PRIVACY INFORMATION MANAGEMENT?

'Privacy' is a term that is being increasingly used in life – but its meaning is not well understood. Wikipedia[1] describes it as "the ability of an individual or group to seclude themselves, or information about themselves, and thereby express themselves selectively".

This guide to ISO/IEC 27701 focuses on the 'information' aspects of privacy. Hence, a privacy information management system (PIMS) deals with the processing of personal information – typically by organisations that an individual deals with.

How you and the organisations that you deal with look after your personal information and allow others to use it without adversely affecting your privacy is a matter for concern. Examples of this issue are discussed below.

Example one

You do not want other people to use your personal information without your permission. This means limiting access to your personal information, and thus keeping it confidential.

This makes good sense, and initially may seem to be the only thing that matters. However, if restricting access to your personal information is all that matters, you could have it stored in a totally sealed iron box. Not very useful when you want an organisation to use it for your benefit!

Example two

You want to be able to share your personal information with an organisation when it will be to your advantage. This means you value the availability of your personal information. You also

---

[1] *https://en.wikipedia.org/wiki/Privacy*.

need it to be available in a usable format and timely manner, and not be used to your disadvantage.

This also makes good sense. We have identified that in controlling our personal information, we need to consider both restricting access to it (an appropriate degree of confidentiality) and ensuring this is balanced with a suitable degree of availability.

Example three

When providing your personal information, you do not – at least when first dealing with a new organisation – know how they will use it or with whom they will share it. Most people are content to rely on the organisation's reputation. Nonetheless, you value the fact that you are confident in dealing with the chosen organisation, i.e. you value the trustworthiness of the services that you receive.

So, with personal information, there is value in knowing where it is stored and how it is being used, having it accessible when needed, knowing what is being retained and being confident that it will be in a format that can be used.

Thus, when referring to privacy information management, this is not only about the security aspects of the personal information (which deals with confidentiality, integrity and availability) but also about the who, where, how, what and why of the management of personal information.

Organisations wish to manage the personal information that they process in a way that ensures their clients and customers can be confident that their privacy is protected. This is often achieved by setting up management arrangements that introduce a set of policies, processes and working arrangements that help them exercise the degree of control required to provide the necessary assurances. Such arrangements are generically described as a PIMS – this is the focus of ISO/IEC 27701.

Who does it matter to?

Privacy information management (defined as the protection of privacy) is affected by the processing of personal information. This processing is subdivided in a number of different ways by the legislation and regulation applicable in different jurisdictions. As an example, within the European Union, by the EU General Data Protection Regulation (GDPR) into six data protection principles:

1. Processing shall be fair and lawful, and for specific purposes.

2. Processing shall not be used for any other purpose.

3. Personal information shall be adequate and relevant for the specified purposes, and shall be limited to what is needed for the purposes.

4. Personal information shall be accurate and where necessary up to date.

5. Personal information shall not be retained for longer than is necessary.

6. Personal information shall be processed in a secure manner.

It is obvious that it is not just the personal information itself that we need to be concerned with, but its collection, storage, handling, sharing/transferring and processing. When considering all of these processes, it is easy to conclude that every organisation should be concerned with their privacy information management arrangements.

Individuals are referred to by legislation as 'data subjects'; this can include members of the public, customers and staff. These individuals will want to know that their personal information is being managed and protected appropriately. Security breaches can result in the disclosure of large volumes of personal information to criminal hackers, which in turn can result in a loss of trust in the organisations that suffer the breaches.[2]

Organisations in the private sector will be driven by a number of factors, including client and customer requirements, compliance with legal and regulatory requirements, and the need to remain competitive. Public-sector organisations have similar drivers to maintain a strong privacy management stance and safeguard against privacy-related incidents.

Where matters!

It is worth noting that not all countries operate the same levels of privacy protection. While the European Union has the GDPR, there is scope within this regulation for countries to operate some of their own rules and regulations. As an example, the EU GDPR talks about charging "a reasonable fee" for a subject access request. The fee-charging regime is set by the local supervisory authority (in the UK, this is the Information Commissioner (IC)). In the UK, there is the Data Protection Act (DPA) 2018[3], and the UK GDPR which is Regulation (EU) 2016/679 of the European Parliament and of the Council of 27 April 2016 on the protection of natural persons with regard to the processing of personal data and on the free movement of such data. In June 2025, the UK Data (Use and Access) Act 2025 received royal assent and will come into force once the commencement orders have been approved.

What this means for individuals is that they need to know where their personal information is being processed. They may also need to be concerned about the location of any other organisations with which their personal information is shared.

---

[2] For example, British Airways suffered a "malicious" data breach in 2018: *https://www.bbc.co.uk/news/uk-england-london-45440850*.

[3] The UK Data Protection Act 2018 will be amended by the UK Data (Use and Access) Act 2025 on commencement (date not available at the time of publication).

How is processing managed?

In many cases, individuals will assume that the organisation that they are sharing their personal information with will be processing it on its own systems. However, with the increasing trend towards relying on business partners for key services and processes, organisations will need policies and agreements to be in place for any sub-contracted processing of personal information (especially Cloud-based service providers). Organisations may need to disclose to their stakeholders the location and contractual arrangements for any such sub-contracted processing.

Outsourcing and other contracts are now increasingly specifying compliance with some form of information governance regime as mandatory.[4]

What is 'personal information'?

The term 'personal information' needs clarifying. A number of terms that have the same or similar meanings are used in different jurisdictions. The UK Data Protection Act (DPA) 2018 and the EU GDPR use the term 'personal data', whereas some jurisdictions (typically in the US) use 'personally identifiable information' (PII). 'Sensitive personal information' (SPI) is also used. For the purposes of this guide, 'personal information' will be used as a catch-all, and in place of where ISO/IEC 27701:2025 uses personally identifiable information or PII.

So, what is this 'personal information'? The EU GDPR defines it as "any information relating to an identified or identifiable natural person" – this is a very wide definition and can be interpreted in a number of ways. The term 'identifiable' brings in the notion of the indirect identification of an individual, using information that the organisation either has on its own systems or can obtain from other sources. With the advent of the Data

---

[4] More on what assurances such schemes provide and on how to interpret any claims is provided in Chapter 6.

(Use and Access) Act 2025, this definition will be updated to "any information relating to a living individual".

Practically, information such as name, address, date of birth, membership number, bank details and physical characteristics can all be taken as personal information. Other information, such as postcode, educational achievements and society membership, can sometimes be included within the definition, depending on what other information is available to the organisation.

Why is personal information being processed?

The main reason for the processing of personal information by organisations is the need to deliver the appropriate services to the individual. Having said that, the amount of personal information being processed will typically depend on the services being offered. A bank will need to be very sure that it is dealing with the individual concerned, and thus will need verifiable and accurate personal information. On the other hand, a train company selling tickets for specific journeys may not need to know any personal information about the individual they are carrying.

Another key driver is the need to maintain a competitive edge. The obvious objective of not allowing competitors access to the personal information that you process falls within the remit of personal information management, as are the less obvious benefits of effective privacy management such as improvements in customer service through appropriately managed databases (e.g. no longer sending mailshots to addresses that the client has told you they have moved from).

An effective personal information management regime can provide an organisation with the foundations on which to build a knowledge management strategy and realise the true value of all the personal information that it holds, provided of course that the organisation has obtained the necessary consents from the individuals concerned.

The public sector has its own drivers, including issues such as justice and national security, as well as the responsibility to become as effective and efficient as possible in conducting its work to be able to truly demonstrate appropriate stewardship of public funds.

To all this should be added the obvious requirement that staff from any organisation will expect their personal information to be managed appropriately and their right to privacy respected.

CHAPTER 2: WHAT NEEDS TO BE CONSIDERED?

So, how can an effective privacy information management system (PIMS) address the needs of an organisation? What needs to be addressed? Does this include issues relating to clients and customers, staff at all levels, suppliers and cultural issues? What must also be considered is that privacy information management goes well beyond the remit of information technology, as personal information in any medium (such as hard copy) needs to be included in the organisation's PIMS. The organisation would also benefit if the PIMS covers the whole of the organisation and its sub-contractors.

Having identified what privacy information management is, and recognising it as something that organisations need to be concerned about, the next stage is to determine exactly what areas and aspects of the organisation will be affected.

ISO/IEC 27701 introduces a number of terms and phrases. It talks about needing to consider the "external and internal issues" that are likely to affect the organisation and its business. The obvious external issue is the need to be able to demonstrate how legal and regulatory requirements related to the management of personal information are complied with. As legislation such as the EU GDPR and the UK DPA typically talk about outcomes (e.g. being fair to the data subject) rather than detailed processes, how the necessary outcomes are achieved will be reliant upon good organisational procedures.

Internal issues will largely relate to staff management and reporting. Every member of staff (including external consultants and sub-contractors) who handles personal information will need to know what they must (and must not) do with that personal information. And, of course, this extends beyond the personal information about clients/customers and may well include personal information about other members of staff and related third parties.

Another term used in ISO/IEC 27701 is 'interested parties'. This includes, among others, company directors (who are responsible for compliance with applicable legislation and regulations), regulators such as (in the UK) the Information Commissioner, and clients/customers of the organisation. All these interested parties need to be confident that the PIMS is relevant to the organisation and provides the appropriate assurances.

ISO/IEC 27701 thus requires that the external and internal factors are determined by the organisation, and that the intended outcomes are achieved. The following factors are included:

- Applicable legislation and regulations.
- Judicial decisions.
- Organisational context.
- Contractual requirements.

These all need to be taken into account when developing or improving the PIMS. Typically, everything that is related to the processing of personal information (which includes processes such as capture, storage, updating and disposal) needs to be included in the PIMS: all the equipment on which the personal information is stored (including IT systems and hard copy files), how it is moved/transmitted (file transfers, email and other messaging systems, social media, etc.), and any aspects of the business that can affect the personal information, the equipment upon which it is processed and the individual processes concerned.

Often there are conflicting pressures on how personal information is processed. Organisations may wish to leverage the personal information that they process to, for example, expand their client base. On the other hand, the data subjects involved may not have given permission for this activity to take place. Organisations will need to balance their own needs with the wishes of the individuals concerned to ensure that compliance with legislation and regulations is not compromised. Thus, the dependencies and interfaces of all aspects of the management system and the personal information it controls must be considered. In particular, to reduce the risk of inappropriate processing occurring, information security measures need to be developed and implemented. This includes when personal information is transmitted to another office of the same organisation or to a sub-contractor, when the selection of the transmission processes and the security requirements placed on the transmission are key.

As far as the 'interested parties' are concerned, ISO/IEC 27701 says that their needs and expectations need to be understood by the organisation. Where the interested party is an individual, they will expect the organisation to protect their privacy. Such protection can take many forms, including only retaining the personal information needed for the organisation's operations, removing it from its systems when it is no longer needed, and protecting it from deliberate and/or accidental activities that would compromise interested parties' expectations.

As noted above, the format of the personal information and the media on which it is stored are of prime importance. The PIMS should consider all the different formats and media that are in use, and ensure that the appropriate mechanisms are in place. When personal information is in transit – whether it be in the form of papers being taken home for reviewing the night before a meeting, or electronic records being sent to a third party for processing – it becomes obvious that hard-copy documents warrant a similar degree of protection to electronic versions. If personal information is accessed by a competitor, it does not matter whether it is in an email attachment or printed on a piece of paper: the personal information that was meant to be kept confidential has been accessed in an unauthorised manner, and thus a potential privacy breach. Where such a breach might have a negative effect on the data subject, the onus is on the organisation to protect the individual concerned, and may result in legal sanctions, compensation claims and/or loss of confidence in the organisation concerned.

When dealing with sub-contractors (data processors), consideration needs to be given to all the above points. These sub-contractors are (in effect) extensions to the organisation, so any inappropriate activities carried out by the sub-contractor that affect the processing of the personal information should be considered activities of the organisation itself. Hence, the organisation's relationship with its sub-contractors (and there could be many of these, including sub-contractors in other countries) is vital. The ability to understand the systems and processes employed by sub-contractors, and where necessary audit these systems and processes, is one of the important aspects to be considered when choosing sub-contracting partners.

CHAPTER 3: ISO/IEC 27701 AND THE PRIVACY INFORMATION MANAGEMENT SYSTEM REQUIREMENTS

As with most topics, there are international standards that deal with the discipline of privacy management. The key standards for privacy management are as follows:

- ISO/IEC 27701:2025 is the international standard for privacy information management.[5] It contains the requirements and provides guidance for a privacy information management system (PIMS).

- ISO/IEC 29100 provides a privacy framework. This standard gives common privacy terminology, defines the actors and their roles in processing personally identifiable information (PII), describes privacy safeguarding requirements and details 11 privacy principles.

There are other standards that provide guidance on many of the topics ISO/IEC 27701 raises. These are some of the most relevant:

- ISO/IEC 20889 – *Privacy enhancing data de-identification terminology and classification of techniques*.

- ISO/IEC 27018 – *Guidelines for protection of personally identifiable information (PII) in public clouds acting as PII processors*.

- ISO/IEC TR 27550 – *Privacy engineering for system life cycle processes*.

---

[5] Other standards that have been used in referencing privacy information management include BS 10012 in the UK – first published in 2009.

- ISO/IEC 27555 – *Guidelines on personally identifiable information deletion.*

- ISO/IEC 27556 – *User-centric privacy preferences management framework.*

- ISO/IEC 27557 – *Application of ISO 31000:2018 for organizational privacy risk management.*

- ISO/IEC 27559 – *Privacy enhancing data de-identification framework.*

- ISO/IEC 27560 – *Consent record information structure.*

- ISO/IEC 27562 – *Privacy guidelines for fintech services.*

- ISO/IEC TS 27570 – *Privacy guidelines for smart cities.*

- ISO/IEC 27706 – *Requirements for bodies providing audit and certification of privacy information management systems.*

- ISO/IEC 29101 – *Privacy architecture framework.*

- ISO/IEC 29134 – *Guidelines for privacy impact assessment.*

- ISO/IEC 29151 – *Code of practice for personally identifiable information protection.*

- ISO/IEC 29190 – *Privacy capability assessment model.*

One of the challenges of ISO/IEC 27701 is the variation of the definition of privacy information processing around the world. Indeed, the definition of personal information differs internationally. The ISO/IEC committee that develops privacy-related standards (ISO/IEC JTC1/SC27/WG5) has decided on the term 'personally identifiable information' (see ISO/IEC 29100 for a definition) – ISO/IEC 27701 uses this term. The EU GDPR uses the term 'personal data'. To address this issue,

ISO/IEC 27701 allows users to adopt local definitions for their own implementations.

ISO/IEC 27701 sets out the requirements for establishing a PIMS through to its review and continual improvement and adaptation to the changing environment in which the organisation implementing the PIMS operates.

As with other management system standards, ISO/IEC 27701:2025 is aligned to the recognised Plan-Do-Check-Act (PDCA) model of continual improvement, a means of designing, developing and implementing an effective PIMS. While this is not strictly mandated by ISO/IEC 27701, it remains one valid and effective approach.

The PDCA cycle can be summarised as:

- **Plan** what you need to do to achieve the objective (which includes defining what that objective is);

- **Do** what you planned;

- **Check** that what you have done achieves what you had planned for it to achieve and identify any gaps or shortfalls (i.e. check whether you have met the objectives); and

- **Act** on the findings of the check phase to address the gaps and/or improve the efficiency and effectiveness of what you have in place.

Typically, this last stage will involve making a plan to further refine and enhance the PIMS to reflect the changing expectations of interested parties, doing what that plan entails, checking that the objectives were achieved, identifying any shortfalls and then acting on the findings by once again creating a plan.

Therefore, with the introduction of a PIMS using PDCA, the initial cycle of continual improvement is achieved. In practice, other PDCA cycles are instigated that progress to different timelines in parallel.

One common misunderstanding in adopting the PDCA approach is that the planning stage is limited purely to planning the project. However, the planning stage includes all the activity to determine what is required of the PIMS, and how this is to be achieved. This is a huge undertaking, to the extent that it can take a significant proportion of the project time from initiation through to having a full PIMS in place. The other main resource-demanding stage is implementation. The next chapter deals with the most resource-intensive aspects of determining what is required of the PIMS.

As an ISO standard, ISO/IEC 27701 is written in accordance with the ISO procedures for management system standards, hence the requirements for a PIMS defined in ISO/IEC 27701 adopt the same high-level structure[6] and much of the core text of other management system standards. This includes the following requirements that provide an effective foundation for any management system.

Documentation

It is important, both in the short and long term, to be able to demonstrate how the corporate policies, operating procedures and work instructions were formulated. The organisation is likely to find it useful to retain records of developments and activities upon which it can call should it need to in the future. Hence the requirement that many of these items are recorded and that the organisation retains appropriate records for as long as necessary.

It is also important to create records of operating activities, for the purposes of review and decision making. These records may include audit trail data, both in manual and automated forms.

---

[6] The separation of ISO/IEC 27701:2025 from ISO/IEC 27001 should ensure implementers and auditors recognise and ensure the important topics of leadership, planning, support and continual improvement for the management of personal information that have always been required are given due attention. This is an area that was often overlooked previously.

The records need to be safeguarded once created, by ensuring that only the appropriate (authorised) people have access to them when needed, and that the integrity of their contents can be demonstrated.

Operating procedures need to describe the processes that support the corporate policies and explain who does what, where and when.

Work instructions might be introduced to detail how certain tasks are carried out.

All documentation needs to have been written and approved by the right people, and the organisation must ensure that only the latest approved versions are available to those who need to be aware of and follow them.

There is also a requirement that documents sourced externally are subject to control where appropriate, including those created by AI solutions.

Now, let's return to the common management system 'hygiene' factors, and audit.

Audit

Audits can be undertaken at either an internal or external level.

The auditing of management systems in general (and a PIMS in particular) has the objective of demonstrating that the management system conforms to the organisation's requirements, conforms to the requirements of the appropriate international standard, and is effectively implemented and maintained.

Internal audits can be used for many purposes, but one of the main objectives of deploying an internal management system audit programme is to monitor compliance between the management system requirements and working practice. Internal management system audits are commissioned by the organisation, for the organisation, and provide an opportunity to review the level of conformity within, and effectiveness of, the PIMS. This is achieved by examining what happens across a sample of activities and processes and comparing this to what the management system describes. The identification of any mismatch provides the opportunity to correct it, either by changing the system description of what happens, enhancing working practices or addressing competency issues (often through further training and awareness). The internal audit process should also inform the continual improvement of the PIMS. However, this typically only becomes an objective of audits once the PIMS is embedded.

Internal audits can be resourced either by an organisation's audit function, by individuals who are familiar with audit programmes and can act independently of the processes and arrangements they are auditing, or externally by specialist auditors. Typically, audits involve the selection of one or more processes and checking actual practice against requirements. Audit reports will identify any non-conformances between the actual practice and the requirements. The organisation will need to review any identified non-conformances and make the appropriate adjustments, either to the work practices or, where it is within their remit, the requirement(s).

Audits also provide the opportunity for improvement. Therefore, audit programmes and audit programme objectives can include the identification of potential improvements to the PIMS. This could include updates to policy (perhaps prompted by changes to legislation/regulations and their interpretation that had not been accommodated in the PIMS before the internal audit), operating procedures and/or work instructions.

Internal audits can also be commissioned to target specific areas of concern or to identify opportunities for improvement.

Management review

Top management (defined in management system terms as a 'person or group of people who directs and controls an organisation at the highest level' – where the organisation is that in scope of the PIMS) has a significant role in the management of a management system, and this applies equally to a PIMS. Management initiates the development of the management system, approves the resource necessary to develop and maintain it, and approves corporate policies that define the objectives of the management system.

It is therefore appropriate that top management reviews the progress of the PIMS from its inception through to operation, ensuring that it is effective and meets corporate requirements, over time.

It is appropriate to carry out management reviews at regular intervals (such as every 12 months) to achieve these objectives. These reviews could consider audit reports (from internal, supplier and external audits), any changes to legislation/regulations, any privacy-related incidents, and suggestions from operational staff. The review could also examine the effectiveness measures[7] that have been developed and any opportunities for continual improvement that have been identified or implemented.

The arrangements for document control and continual improvement can be introduced at the outset of a PIMS project, providing arrangements to support the project and to ensure familiarity with any changes to working practices that need to continue once the initial project has delivered and as the PIMS becomes part of business as usual. Organisations that already have these arrangements in place could review them to ensure they meet the requirements of ISO/IEC 27701:2025 and that they are implemented effectively.

---

[7] ISO/IEC 27701:2025 requires the organisation to define how the effectiveness of the PIMS will be measured (including in sections 5.1, 6.1.1.b, 7.2 and 9.1) and for management to consider the measures (section 9.3.1).

Annexes in ISO/IEC 27701

There are a number of annexes (both normative and informative – normative typically being mandatory and informative providing guidance) in ISO/IEC 27701.

Annex A

This annex lists the privacy and security controls. Table A.1 is specifically for organisations acting as data controllers and Table A.2 is specifically for organisations acting as data processors. Table A.3 lists the security considerations that are applicable to both data controllers and data processors. Chapter 5 of this pocket guide considers these controls, following Chapter 4 that addresses how the required blend of controls is identified.

Annex B

This annex links directly to the privacy and security controls listed in Annex A. The Annex provides guidance on the implementation of each control, and where appropriate incudes additional information that may be useful to the implementation of that control.

Annex C

ISO/IEC 29100 is an international standard that defines the vocabulary in use for ISO/IEC 27701. It also defines 11 privacy principles that have been used in ISO/IEC privacy-related standards for some time. This annex contains a cross-reference mapping from these 11 principles to the controls listed in Annex A of ISO/IEC 27701.

Annex D

The EU GDPR details the legal requirements for the processing of personal data. This annex lists the provisions of ISO/IEC 27701 and how these map to the EU GDPR. It should be noted that all the provisions map to the EU GDPR, and that each requirement of the EU GDPR (Articles 5 to 49 except 43[8]) can be mapped to the provisions in ISO/IEC 27701.

Annex E

There are two international standards that provide information for those involved in the processing of personal information:

- ISO/IEC 27018 gives further information for the protection of PII in public Clouds that act as PII processors.
- ISO/IEC 29151 gives additional controls and guidance for the processing of personal information by data controllers.

A mapping of both of these standards is included in this annex to enable easier cross-referencing.

Annex F

This annex gives information about how to transition from ISO/IEC 27701:2019 to the new publication. The annex includes two tables. The first (Table F.1) lists the control identifiers in the current document and links this directly to the identical control identifier in ISO/IEC 27701:2019. The second table (Table F.2) reverses this sequence, allowing an identifier in ISO/IEC 27701:2019 to be linked to the identical control identifier in the new publication.

---

[8] Article 43 is about certification bodies, so is not relevant to ISO/IEC 27701.

CHAPTER 4: LEGAL, REGULATORY AND CONTRACTUAL REQUIREMENTS AND BUSINESS RISK

ISO/IEC 27701 requires an organisation to determine its privacy needs and expectations based on its interested parties – from stakeholders to staff to customers, the public and data subjects – and their expectations for privacy. These requirements, together with the organisation's specific legal, regulatory and contractual obligations, form the starting point for the identification and selection of the appropriate privacy information management system (PIMS) privacy controls. These are combined with the results of a privacy information risk assessment to determine the blend of privacy controls on which the organisation will rely.

As noted earlier, the processing of personal information is covered in most countries by legislation and/or regulations. Hence, any processing needs to be carried out within the local rules. Further, where the organisation is acting as a data processor, contractual requirements will be in place that dictate how the organisation is to act to ensure that the local rules are not compromised.

Thus, the specific requirements of a PIMS need to be determined in light of the appropriate local rules and contractual requirements. These requirements will need to be devised by the organisation, using whatever resources are available. This could include:

- Top management;
- Data protection officer (DPO) or other similar legal expertise;
- Senior operational staff;
- Records management;
- Human resources;
- Information security;

- Technical IT expertise;
- Risk management; and
- Sales and marketing.

Top management will need to be included so that corporate direction (in the form of corporate policies) can be devised and agreed.

Legal expertise will need to be up to date with current legislation and regulations in all the countries that the organisation covers. In some countries, some organisations are required to employ (either internal or external) a suitably qualified individual to cover this legal expertise, referenced in the EU GDPR by the term 'data protection officer[9]'.

Senior operational staff will need to provide input on the operating procedures being used, and how these implement the corporate policies.

Those with records management responsibilities will know how records are captured/created within the organisation, where they are stored and the appropriate retention periods.

Human resources will need to be involved if the processing of personal information related to employees is within the scope of the PIMS. HR will understand what personal information it holds, how it is managed and for how long it is retained.

Information security and/or IT will be aware of the systems being used to manage the personal information, and how it is secured from unauthorised access.

Sales and marketing will have their own needs for personal information. They need to be involved to ensure that their requirements are met by the PIMS.

---

[9] Once the Data (Use and Access) Act 2025 is commenced, the term 'senior responsible individual' replaces 'data protection officer' in the UK.

4: Legal, regulatory and contractual requirements and business risk

ISO/IEC 27701 does not dictate a particular methodology for devising and implementing a PIMS, and in particular for the implementation of a privacy impact assessment (PIA). There are a number of publications giving advice about PIA processes, including guidance from the Information Commissioner.[10]

The objective of a PIA is to identify and minimise the risks to personal information that is involved in a project. It is typically undertaken before the implementation of a project. In the UK, the Information Commissioner states that a PIA is required "for processing that is likely to result in a high risk to individuals". They are recommended as good practice for all processing of personal information.

For the PIA to be effective, it is necessary to consider everything that might go wrong with respect to the processing of personal information – this will need to include the information itself, information processing and storage equipment (every server, computer, laptop, PDA, mobile phone), systems, staff, buildings, etc.

The particular privacy control profile a PIMS provides for an organisation is aligned to its business activities and objectives, and this is determined through the management of privacy risks.

Risk management professionals will understand the risk profile of the organisation, and be able to give risk management advice where necessary. Risk management staff, in conjunction with the legal expertise described earlier, ought to be able to carry out the privacy risk assessments required by ISO/IEC 27701 and any necessary PIAs,[11] sometimes called a data protection impact assessment (DPIA), to determine the necessary privacy controls on which the organisation will rely.

---

[10] *https://ico.org.uk/for-organisations/law-enforcement/guide-to-le-processing/accountability-and-governance/data-protection-impact-assessments/.*
[11] See, for example, ISO/IEC 29134. Some countries have legal requirements for PIAs, particularly when developing new processes that involve personal information.

ISO/IEC 27701 does not dictate a particular methodology for the privacy risk assessment and there are many to choose from. What follows here is a general description of a privacy risk assessment you might expect to see in an effective PIMS.

To undertake the privacy risk assessment, it is necessary to have defined the scope of the PIMS. This is achieved by identifying the relevant issues and requirements of interested parties and the business activities that the PIMS is to encompass. The boundary of the PIMS can then be determined, along with the interfaces and dependencies of the PIMS, with activities undertaken by others outside of the scoped organisation.

For the risk assessment to be effective, the organisation must consider everything that might go wrong with respect to the personal information the PIMS is intended to safeguard – this should consider the privacy principles described in ISO/IEC 29100. The reliance on suppliers and others that can affect the organisation's privacy arrangements will also need to be considered.

Privacy risks need to be identified and the consequence of each coming to fruition estimated in a manner whereby the results of the assessment are comparable and reproducible. The 'consequence' assigned to each risk reflects the total cost to the organisation if that risk were to materialise, including the cost of disruption and recovery, the consequences for the process(es) and products/services, the impact on the organisation's reputation and the consequences for the data subjects affected. The loss of privacy for data subjects can manifest itself in many ways, including increased spam, additional marketing, abuse, and loss of confidence by the individual.

This is normally best estimated by those involved in the relevant business processes.

These consequence values provide the impact aspect of the classic relationship:

$$\textbf{Risk} = \textbf{Likelihood} \times \textbf{Impact}$$

4: Legal, regulatory and contractual requirements and business risk

ISO 27701:2025 defines risk as the *"effect of uncertainty"*.

The risk assessment then uses these estimates, and those of the likelihood of the risk coming to fruition, to determine the risk values. The relationship between likelihood, impact and risk is demonstrated in the following diagram, in this case showing three levels of likelihood and three levels of impact, which together give five levels of risk ranging from 'very low' to 'very high'.

The main aim of a PIMS is to manage all risks to a consistent level, and management needs to determine what level of risk is acceptable. For example, management may, using the diagram in figure 1, decide that risks up to and including 'low' are acceptable, and therefore it is only those risks that have been assessed as falling above that level of 'risk acceptance criteria' that need managing.

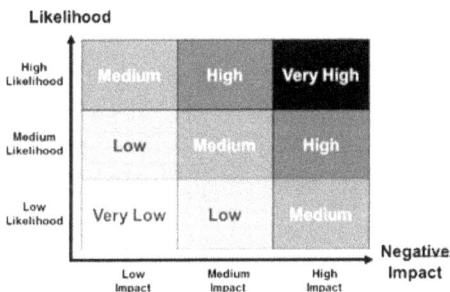

Figure 1: Relationship between likelihood, impact and risk

Defining the gradations on the impact and likelihood scales informs what a 'low risk' equates to, and helps ensure the assessed risks are comparable and reproducible.

Typically, organisations view privacy risks in many different ways. Those that process large quantities of personal information will want to ensure the likelihood of a breach is as low as possible.

On the other hand, organisations that hold small quantities of less sensitive personal information may view the additional security measures as unnecessary, and hence accept an increased risk of privacy breaches occurring.

The organisation's particular level of risk acceptance, its risk appetite or the degree of risk that it is happy to live with on a day-to-day basis, will need to be agreed.

Each risk is assigned to a risk owner, who will be responsible for approving the risk treatment and accepting any residual risk, in light of the risk acceptance criteria.

If a privacy breach should occur, steps need to be taken to address the breach, and where practical the recurrence of the breach needs to be avoided. In the UK, some (more serious) privacy breaches need to be notified to the individual concerned, and to the Information Commissioner. It is thus appropriate that processes are in place to identify privacy breaches, assess their impact (on both the individual and the organisation) and deal with any required notifications.

Applying PIMS controls

Risks assessed as falling above the acceptable level are considered and a decision taken as to what to do about each of them. This decision determines which one or more of the following options to apply to address the identified risk:

- Apply mitigating controls to reduce the risk. (Treat)

- Accept the risk; this is normally determined by the risk acceptance criteria, but can occasionally be applied even if the risk level is above the acceptable level. (Tolerate)

- Avoid the risk by identifying a workaround that negates the risk. (Terminate)

- Transfer the business risk to an insurer or a supplier. (Transfer)

Determining the appropriate treatment and control(s) to manage risk is critical to the performance of the PIMS. The controls can and should be taken from any valid source appropriate to the organisation or process, including designing them yourself.

As different decisions and controls are selected for application to various risks, the risk assessment is re-estimated, and this process continues until all the assessed risks are estimated to meet the risk acceptance criteria.

To ensure that the required level of assurance against privacy risks occurring is achieved, the PIMS controls identified and effectively implemented should be such that the PIMS meets legal, regulatory and contractual obligations.

ISO/IEC 27701 requires that you compare the list of controls determined as necessary to those in ISO/IEC 27701:2025 Annex A and the sections relevant to the role of the processing of personal information within the scope of the PIMS. This ensures that none have been inappropriately omitted and indicates how effective your privacy risk management process has been.

Further information on these controls can be found in Chapter 5.

ISO/IEC 27701 requires a document to be produced that details which controls are required within the PIMS and which are not. This is known as the 'Statement of Applicability' (SoA) – it states which controls are, or are not, applied within the PIMS.

The process to determine the right blend of privacy information controls within the PIMS requires a degree of central coordination, and often benefits from a suitable software solution that can automate many of the potentially resource-intensive administration aspects. ISO/IEC 27701 requires that the privacy risk assessment is reviewed regularly and if significant changes occur. Having software that maintains audit trails of changes and updates to risk estimates helps hugely and addresses one of the tasks necessary even as the PIMS becomes part of business-as-usual (BAU).

CHAPTER 5: PRIVACY INFORMATION MANAGEMENT CONTROLS

Having gained an appreciation of the methodical approach to the selection of privacy information management controls and other ways of addressing risks, it is time to examine the reference control set provided in ISO/IEC 27701:2025.

There are 31 controls in Annex A that relate to data controllers (Table A.1), and 18 controls that relate to data processors (Table A.2). Security considerations, which are appropriate for both data controllers and data processors, are listed in 29 controls (Table A.3).

The controls in Tables A.1 and A.2 are split into four categories:

1. Conditions for collection and processing.
2. Obligations to PII principals.
3. Privacy by design and by default.
4. PII sharing, transfer and disclosure.

These categories are not themselves significant and they could easily be formed differently.

The controls in Table A.3 are all in one category, and are largely taken from ISO/IEC 27001:2022.

ISO/IEC 27701 emphasises that the controls it details in Annex A are to be used to ensure that none have been inappropriately omitted and that they are not a default control set that organisations have to use. Typically, an organisation would start with sector- and contract-specific requirements and then consider others. There will also be technological developments that introduce risks that are not covered to a suitable extent by the security controls listed in Annex A of ISO/IEC 27701, so it may be necessary to adopt further controls.

Implementation guidance

Annex B of ISO/IEC 27701 documents implementation guidance aligned to the controls in Annex A. Hence, the guidance in B.1.2.2 relates to the control in Table A.1, A.1.2.2.

Controls for data controllers

The following table lists the privacy controls applicable to data controllers:

Control reference	Control title
A.1.2.2	Identify and document purpose
A.1.2.3	Identify lawful basis
A.1.2.4	Determine when and how consent is to be obtained
A.1.2.5	Obtain and record consent
A.1.2.6	Privacy impact assessment
A.1.2.7	Contracts with PII processors
A.1.2.8	Joint PII controller
A.1.2.9	Records related to processing PII
A.1.3.2	Determining and fulfilling obligations to PII principals
A.1.3.3	Determining information for PII principals
A.1.3.4	Providing information to PII principals
A.1.3.5	Providing mechanism to modify or withdraw consent

Control reference	Control title
A.1.3.6	Providing mechanism to object to PII processing
A.1.3.7	Access, correction or erasure
A.1.3.8	PII controllers' obligations to inform third parties
A.1.3.9	Providing copy of PII processed
A.1.3.10	Handling requests
A.1.3.11	Automated decision making
A.1.4.2	Limit collection
A.1.4.3	Limit processing
A.1.4.4	Accuracy and quality
A.1.4.5	PII minimization objectives
A.1.4.6	PII de-identification and deletion at the end of processing
A.1.4.7	Temporary files
A.1.4.8	Retention
A.1.4.9	Disposal
A.1.4.10	PII transmission controls
A.1.5.2	Identify basis for PII transfer between jurisdictions
A.1.5.3	Countries and international organizations to which PII can be transferred

Control reference	Control title
A.1.5.4	Records of transfer of PII
A.1.5.5	Records of PII disclosures to third parties

Controls for data processors

The following table lists the privacy controls applicable to data processors:

Control reference	Control title
A.2.2.2	Customer agreement
A.2.2.3	Organization's purposes
A.2.2.4	Marketing and advertising use
A.2.2.5	Infringing instruction
A.2.2.6	Customer obligations
A.2.2.7	Records related to processing PII
A.2.3.2	Comply with obligations to PII principals
A.2.4.2	Temporary files
A.2.4.3	Return, transfer or disposal of PII
A.2.4.4	PII transmission controls
A.2.5.2	Basis for PII transfer between jurisdictions

Control reference	Control title
A.2.5.3	Countries and international organizations to which PII can be transferred
A.2.5.4	Records of PII disclosures to third parties
A.2.5.5	Notification of PII disclosure requests
A.2.5.6	Legally binding PII disclosures
A.2.5.7	Disclosure of subcontractors used to process PII
A.2.5.8	Engagement of a subcontractor to process PII
A.2.5.9	Change of subcontractor to process PII

Conditions for collection and processing

For data controllers, this category includes many of the main controls off which the rest of the system hangs. There is a need for corporate-level controls related to how and why personal information is collected and processed. This includes the identification and documentation of the lawful purposes for which personal information is collected, based on the organisation's privacy impact assessment (PIA). Where the lawful basis is identified as the consent of the data subject, how this consent was obtained and what information about the processing was provided at the time to the data subject must be recorded.

This category also includes the management of the relationship with any data processors, and how processing is managed where joint data controllers are involved.

For data processors, this category deals with the relationship with the data controller, including the assurance that the personal information being processed is not used for purposes outside the agreement with the data controller.

The controls for data controllers in this section are:

- The identification and documentation of the purposes for which personal information will be processed (A.1.2.2);

- The identification and documentation of the lawful basis for the processing (A.1.2.3);

- Where consent is the lawful basis, the identification and recording of how this consent is obtained (A.1.2.4 and A.1.2.5);

- The results of a PIA where this is deemed necessary (A.1.2.6);

- Where a data processor is used, the development and approval of an appropriate written contract (A.1.2.7);

- Where a joint data controller relationship is identified, the documentation of the roles and responsibilities of the parties involved (A.1.2.8); and

- The creation and retention of the appropriate records of the processing of personal information.

Hence, for each process that an organisation implements, and which includes the processing of personal information, there needs to be a justifiable reason each piece of information is being processed. For example [Example 1], organisations with employees will process information related to those employees, for the purposes of managing their employment (including the payment of remuneration). In this example, the employee information is being held for the performance of an employment contract.

As a second example [Example 2], an organisation is supplying goods or services to individuals. So, information relating to delivery requirements will be processed, for the purpose of performing the sales contract. The question then may be: can the organisation process further information relating to the individual, perhaps for marketing purposes? This situation is often managed by supermarkets by loyalty cards, where in effect the individual consents to the supermarket retaining further information (the purchasing profile) and makes marketing offers to the individual.

The controls for data processors in this section are:

- The development and implementation of processes to monitor the performance of the contract with the data controller (A.2.2.2);

- Ensuring that only those purposes specified in the contract with the data controller are processed (A.2.2.3);

- Ensuring that the personal information being processed within the data controller contract is not used for further marketing and advertising (A.2.2.4);

- Ensuring that the data controller is informed of any instances where legal requirements are (or may be) infringed (A.2.2.5);

- Providing the data controller with information related to the processing as and when required (A.2.2.6); and

- The creation and retention of the appropriate records of the processing of personal information on behalf of the data controller (A.2.2.7).

For Example 1, the data processor may be offering payroll services to the data controller. If an ex-employee asks the data processor directly for information related to their salary payments, the data processor would normally (unless expressly detailed in the data controller/processor contract) promptly inform the data controller of the request.

For Example 2, where the data processor is processing information related to the loyalty card, a similar situation exists to Example 1 when an individual asks the data processor for information relating to their purchasing history.

Obligations to data subjects

For data controllers, this category includes the documentation of their legal and regulatory obligations to data subjects, determining and providing the information that the data subject requires, and providing procedures for the handling of requests from data subjects. These requests can include the correction of inaccurate personal information, providing copies of personal information that is held, and ensuring that any third parties with which the personal information has been shared are kept up to date with any changes to that information.

For data processors, this category is mainly handled by the data controller. Data processors need to ensure that the appropriate data controller can fulfil its legal obligations. This includes dealing with requests from data subjects directed to the data processor; in most cases, this is dealt with by referring the request to the data controller.

The controls for data controllers in this section are:

- The identification, documentation and implementation of their obligations (legal, regulatory and business) to individuals (A.1.3.2);

- The identification and provision of information to individuals about the processing of their personal information (A.1.3.3 and A.1.3.4);

- The provision of processes whereby individuals can modify and/or withdraw their consent to the processing of their personal information (A.1.3.5);

- The provision of processes whereby individuals can object to the processing of their personal information (A.1.3.6);

- The provision of processes whereby individuals can access, correct and/or erase their personal information (A.1.3.7);

- The provision of a process whereby third parties with which personal information has been shared are informed of the modification, withdrawal or erasure of personal information and request the appropriate action (A.1.3.8);

- The provision of processes whereby individuals can receive copies of their personal information on request (A.1.3.9);

- The provision of processes whereby individuals can make legitimate requests relating to the processing of their personal information (A.1.3.10); and

- The provision of processes whereby, where personal information is processed solely by automated processes, individuals can request reviews of the results of these processes by non-automated processes (A.1.3.11).

For Example 1, personal information related to employees changes from time to time (address, bank details, surname). Organisations need processes to keep employee information up to date; they may also need to retain historical information (such as previous addresses).

For Example 2, personal information related to customers with loyalty cards changes from time to time (address, bank details, surname). Organisations might consider that providing web-based systems for individuals to update their own information might be sufficient. Apart from the potential security issues with such processes, a 'non-web-based' process needs to be available for those customers without web facilities.

For both these examples, it is important that the data controller includes appropriate proof of identity processes to ensure that the individual can only make changes to their own personal information (which includes valid requests from third parties that hold powers of attorney).

The control for data processors in this section is:

- The identification, documentation and implementation of procedures to enable the data controller to meet its obligations (A.2.3.2).

As a general example of this control, data processors are tasked with a number of requirements, such as promptly informing the data controller of any data breach (or suspected breach). This includes information about the type of breach, any details of the personal information involved, and any remedial action taken by the data processor.

Privacy by design and by default

For data controllers, this category deals with the implementation of the data minimisation principle. This includes the following:

- Only collect the minimum personal information that is necessary for the intended purpose.
- Only retain personal information for the intended purpose.
- Ensure that the personal information being processed is accurate and up to date.
- Once the intended purpose is completed, dispose of all copies of the personal information held for that purpose.
- Ensure that any temporary files created by processing that include personal information are deleted as soon as possible.
- Ensure that the integrity of any personal information sent to another organisation is protected.

For data processors, this category is mainly covered by the data controller. The data processor will need to abide by the agreement with the data controller, which will include the need to remove all personal information from its systems once the processing is completed.

The controls for data controllers in this section are:

- The limiting of the collection of personal information to the minimum needed for the process involved (A.1.4.2);
- The limiting of the processing of personal information to the minimum needed for the process involved (A.1.4.3);

- The maintaining of the accuracy of the personal information being processed (A.1.4.4);

- The evaluation of existing and proposed processing to ensure that only the minimum personal information is processed (including the use of de-identification techniques where appropriate) (A.1.4.5);

- The removal or de-identification of personal information at the end of the processing (A.1.4.6);

- The removal of temporary files containing personal information to ensure that supplementary copies of personal information are not retained (A.1.4.7);

- The removal or de-identification of personal information at the end of its retention period (A.1.4.8);

- The provision of processes whereby personal information (including all copies) is disposed of in a secure manner (A.1.4.9); and

- The implementation of processes and procedures that ensure that personal information sent over data transmission systems reaches only its intended recipients (A.1.4.10).

For Example 1, where processing relates to payroll systems, only information that is necessary to carry out the payroll task needs to be processed. Further, this information must be kept up to date (especially where the individual requests verifiable changes to that personal information) and all copies of the personal information must be disposed of at the end of the processing (typically when the individual is no longer employed by the data controller).

A similar situation applies to Example 2, especially where loyalty card information for marketing purposes is involved. If an individual identifies out-of-date information about themselves (perhaps due to a change of address), the appropriate action needs to be taken (including the check on the validity of the change) by updating the personal information involved.

The controls for data processors in this section are:

- The removal of temporary files containing personal information to ensure that supplementary copies of personal information are not retained (A.2.4.2);

- The provision of processes whereby personal information (including all copies) is returned, transferred or disposed of in a secure manner, as required by the contract with the data controller (A.2.4.3); and

- The implementation of processes and procedures that ensure that personal information sent over data transmission systems reaches only its intended recipients (A.2.4.4).

Applicable to both examples, this section identifies two issues related to the provision of data processor services:

- During the contract period, processes that ensure that any transmission of information (which includes physical transfers) is only made available to the intended recipient. Hence, security controls and management of identity will need to be configured in an appropriate manner.

- At the end of the contract, all processing (including storage) of personal information related to that contract is terminated, and any transfer of personal information back to the data controller (or as instructed by the data controller) is completed in a secure manner.

Sharing, transfer and disclosure of personal information

For data controllers, this category requires policies and procedures to be in place to ensure that any sharing and/or disclosure of personal information is handled in compliance with legislation and/or regulations. This includes, in particular, the sharing of information with organisations in different countries or with international organisations. To enable data controllers to be able to demonstrate how they deal with this requirement, the appropriate records need to be created and retained.

For data processors, the same requirements as for data controllers are relevant. In addition, where a data processor uses a sub-contractor for some of the processing, the data controller needs to be aware of this, and approve any changes to the sub-contractor.

The controls for data controllers in this section are:

- The identification of the legal basis for transferring personal information to other jurisdictions (A.1.5.2);

- The identification of the jurisdictions to which personal information is transferred (A.1.5.3);

- The creation and retention of records of transfers to other jurisdictions (A.1.5.4); and

- The creation and retention of records of disclosures to third parties of personal information (A.1.5.5).

Where personal information is transferred to other jurisdictions, care needs to be taken to ensure that the privacy expectations of the individuals involved are not compromised. Laws and regulations do vary (sometimes widely) in other jurisdictions, hence the need for care. As an example, legal requirements/regulations in some countries require the disclosure of personal information to crime prevention authorities without reference to the data controller.

The controls for data processors in this section are:

- The identification of the legal basis for transferring personal information to other jurisdictions (A.2.5.2);

- The identification of the jurisdictions to which personal information can be transferred (A.2.5.3);

- The creation and retention of records of transfers to other jurisdictions (A.2.5.4);

- The notification (and rejection where appropriate) of legally binding requests for the disclosure to third parties of personal information (A.2.5.5 and A.2.5.6); and

- The disclosure (and approval where appropriate) to the data controller of any subcontractors used by the data processor, including the approval of any change of subcontractor (A.2.5.7, A.2.5.8 and A.2.5.9).

When data processors are processing personal information on behalf of a data controller, the jurisdiction within which they are located (including the jurisdiction of any subcontractors) needs to be made known to the data controller. This is to ensure that the data controller is aware of any potential issues with safeguarding the privacy of individuals within other jurisdictions.

Security considerations

This category applies equally to data controllers and data processors. The principal objective of the controls in Table A.3 is to ensure the security of the processing of personal information. This includes the development and implementation of information security policies, the allocation of security roles and responsibilities, the classification and labelling of personal information, and the development of appropriate processes and procedures for the ongoing use (including storage) of personal information.

The PIMS information security controls in Annex A.3 have guidance detailed in Annex B clause B.3. The Annex A controls also map to the information security management system standard control set in ISO/IEC 27001:2022 Annex A as detailed in the following table. Each control in ISO/IEC 27001:2022 Annex A is mirrored in ISO/IEC 27002:2022 with guidance on its implementation but without a focus on the protection of personal information.

5: Privacy information management controls

ISO/IEC 27701:2025 Annex A		ISO/IEC 27001:2022 Annex A
Ref.	**Information security control title**	**Ref.**
A.3.3	Policies for information security	5.1
A.3.4	Information security roles and responsibilities	5.2
A.3.5	Classification of information	5.12
A.3.6	Labelling of information	5.13
A.3.7	Information transfer	5.14
A.3.8	Identity management	5.16
A.3.9	Access rights	5.18
A.3.10	Addressing information security within supplier agreements	5.20
A.3.11	Information security incident management planning and preparation	5.24
A.3.12	Response to information security incidents	5.26
A.3.13	Legal, statutory, regulatory and contractual requirements	5.31
A.3.14	Protection of records	5.33

ISO/IEC 27701:2025 Annex A		ISO/IEC 27001:2022 Annex A
Ref.	**Information security control title**	**Ref.**
A.3.15	Independent review of information security	5.35
A.3.16	Compliance with policies, rules and standards for information security	5.36
A.3.17	Information security awareness, education and training	6.3
A.3.18	Confidentiality or non-disclosure agreements	6.6
A.3.19	Clear desk and clear screen	7.7
A.3.20	Storage media	7.10
A.3.21	Secure disposal or re-use of equipment	7.14
A.3.22	User end point devices	8.1
A.3.23	Secure authentication	8.5
A.3.24	Information backup	8.13
A.3.25	Logging	8.15
A.3.26	Use of cryptography	8.24

ISO/IEC 27701:2025 Annex A		ISO/IEC 27001:2022 Annex A
Ref.	**Information security control title**	**Ref.**
A.3.27	Secure development life cycle	8.25
A.3.28	Application security requirements	8.26
A.3.29	Secure system architecture and engineering principles	8.27
A.3.30	Outsourced development	8.30
A.3.31	Test information	8.33

The PIMS controls cover the following, all of which should be determined as being necessary, or not, in accordance with the privacy risk assessment and treatment activity and the context of the organisation, whether a data controller, a data processor or both.

Policies and roles (controls B.3.3 and B.3.4)

These controls require an organisation to develop privacy and information security policies to demonstrate commitment to legal and contractual privacy protection requirements with due regard to legal requirements. The responsibilities for the protection of personal information should be clearly allocated across all relevant parties, internally and externally.

The responsibilities should include an identified contact point for the processing of personal information, including being a contact for individuals where the organisation is a data controller, and suitably qualified personnel should be appointed with responsibility for privacy governance and compliance. The ISO/IEC 27701:2025 guidance includes factors to consider in defining the responsible person and their duties.

Personal information labelling, handling and transfer (controls B.3.5, B.3.6 and B.3.7)

The design and implementation of a classification scheme that identifies categories of personal information, together with clear rules on how each category of classified personal information should be protected and processed, is covered by two controls in ISO/IEC 27701:2025. Ensuring members of staff are familiar with the labelling scheme and its implications for handling the information is key, along with an appreciation of who the information can be shared with once appropriate procedures and agreements are in place – as with other controls, the effectiveness of these arrangements will depend on how they are implemented in parallel with other controls, such as supplier management (control A.3.10) where personal information could be impacted by a supplier.

Identity and access management (A.3.8, A.3.9 and A.3.23)

User and access management require user registration/ deregistration and access to be managed with care. User profiles need to be managed from creation to decommissioning for all roles related to personal information. The guidance indicates that user identifiers should not be reassigned once deactivated and that where other organisations are responsible for user management, the contract with them should make the responsibilities clear.

As with user registration and deregistration, access rights should be assigned, regularly reviewed, revised when appropriate and removed in accordance with a policy. We recommend maintaining a record of access rights and how they vary. The allocation of individual user accounts enables traceability of who did what when appropriate logging (see control A.3.25) is in place.

The benefits of allocating individual user accounts with defined access rights is entwined with secure authentication arrangements (A.3.23) – the means for any users (staff, suppliers and/or customers) to demonstrate they are the appropriate person to use the account without others being able to do the same is essential.

Supplier management (A.3.10)

This control requires the agreement of information security measures with suppliers where they are likely to impact personal information. The commitments should reflect the organisation's information security requirements such as those detailed in data controller–data processor contracts (see control A.1.2.7) and/or customer agreements (control A.2.2.2).

The responsibilities might usefully include the need to report relevant information security breaches (see controls A.3.11 and A.3.12).

Information security incidents (A.3.11 and A.3.12)

Privacy information incidents can take many forms, typically but not exclusively related to security incidents. Security-related breaches are often the result of inappropriate access to personal information. Other types of breaches can be caused by obtaining personal information not required for the related purpose, retaining personal information for longer than is necessary for the related purpose, or not updating personal information that is known to be inaccurate or out of date.

The PIMS controls at A.3.11 and A.3.12 relate to the need for an organisation to plan and prepare for information security incidents related to personal information. These controls are typically factored into the organisation's information security/cyber security breach management arrangements and ensure that the consequence of any breaches for personal information is considered and managed appropriately.

The management of breaches relating to personal information should include a means of determining the extent of reaction and escalation required to effectively manage the issue, and the reporting of incidents to the relevant parties, including supervisory authority(ies), to data controllers (for data processors) and to the individuals the personal data relates to. Records of information security incidents relevant to personal information should be maintained.

Issues that are likely to result in a privacy breach and/or an information security incident are key areas for privacy information management awareness campaigns, as the organisation should be in a position to benefit from notification of a potential problem as soon as possible. Therefore, awareness needs to be raised and maintained for all relevant parties, including data subjects, data processors, suppliers, business partners, customers and staff, on how to report issues when they arise.

Obligations and records (controls A.3.13 and A.3.14)

Identifying and complying with legal and regulatory privacy requirements run throughout ISO/IEC 27701, from considering privacy legislation in setting the context of the PIMS, through privacy risk assessment and privacy risk treatment, to the controls (i.e. the lawful basis for processing of personal information at control A.1.2.3).

The control for legal, statutory, regulatory and contractual requirements (A.3.13) requires the organisation to identify requirements related to personal information and document how it meets them, reviewing the record regularly. The record could usefully include consequences of non-compliance.

It is worth noting here that management system audits cannot be relied upon to demonstrate legal compliance, and as explained in the next chapter, accredited certification to ISO/IEC 27701 does not demonstrate compliance with, say, the EU GDPR; however, first-, second- and third-party audits of a PIMS can be used to demonstrate the intent to comply with relevant legislation and regulations.

The protection of records control (A.3.14) indicates that records of personal information and the processing of it should be safeguarded to ensure they are not lost, falsified, etc. The retention period should align with legislative requirements and the organisation's retention schedules (see control A.1.4.8).

Conformity (A.3.15 and A.3.16)

These controls relate to reviewing compliance with information security rules relating to personal information internally (A.3.16) and having independent confirmation (A.3.15) of the arrangements being appropriate and in place, particularly where interested parties may want assurance that this is the case.

The confirmation of information security arrangements for the protection of personal information is likely to include technical vulnerability tests and monitoring of processing activities.

People factors (A.3.17 and A.3.18)

These two controls align with the human aspects of handling personal information. They address the need for regular information security awareness education and training activities related to each person's role and activities related to the management of personal information, and for confidentiality agreements to be in place with all parties involved with or that could impact the information security of personal information.

The guidance recommends the awareness education and training activities cover the consequences of breaches.

Typically, a confidentiality agreement will include a consequence for breaching it as well as how long the agreement remains in place post-termination of the relationship.

Physical factors (A.3.19, A.3.20, A.3.21 and B.3.22)

The physical security of personal information and the hardware and software it depends on needs to be considered and managed effectively. This includes considering people viewing it on desks or screens, or stealing it whether on paper or on removable storage media such as external hard drives or USB sticks. The management of removable storage media warrants attention across the entire lifecycle of sourcing it through to secure disposal, ensuring that the device is suitably wiped and destroyed. The use of removable media, including what may or may not be stored on it, and the appropriate protection while in transit is likely to dovetail with the controls for the labelling, handling and transfer of information, and that of cryptography. There is also the possibility of re-use of removable media compromising information security that needs to be addressed, ensuring no personal information remains or can be retrieved when assigned to a different user or purpose.

Information backup (A.3.24)

This control recognises that information (and systems) backup relating to personal information is likely to be accommodated in wider information backup arrangements, of course with due regard to any privacy-specific requirements that need to be respected.

The backup and recovery arrangements should ensure the personal-information-relevant systems and the personal information itself are backed up in accordance with any relevant legislation and/or regulation. Arrangements for restoring personal information should ensure that data integrity is maintained and that other measures including access rights, etc. remain in place.

Logs of restores of personal information should be maintained (see protection of records, A.3.14), and the application of retention periods to backup data needs to be considered.

Logging (A.3.25)

IT system logging and monitoring tools can be used to identify processing of personal information outside of the organisation's rules. Alternatively, manual reviews of logs can be deployed when required. The process of generating logs can generate or replicate personal information, so the information produced needs to be considered and managed appropriately, including de-identification of the information and the relevant retention schedule.

Use of cryptography (A.3.26)

This control relates to determining how and where cryptography is to be deployed for managing personal information, the effective management of it and who to communicate this to.

The organisation's cryptography policy should align with legal and regulatory requirements, with levels of encryption being defined for categories of personal information in certain geographies.

Managing information systems (controls A.3.22, A.3.27, A.3.28, A.3.29, A.3.30)

There are five controls that can all be considered as safeguarding information security for personal information in IT systems. Of course, as stated earlier, any of the information security controls rely on and work in tandem with other controls, but for the sake of this chapter we have brigaded these five together:

- Secure development life cycle (A.3.27).

- Application security requirements (A.3.28).

- Secure system architecture and engineering principles (A.3.29).

- Outsourced development (A.3.30).

- User end point devices (A.3.22).

The essence of these controls is that the organisation should determine the information security requirements for protecting personal information it has on its IT systems and ensure those requirements are considered and delivered at every stage of the IT system's lifecycle(s). This means that from the start of considering which IT solutions to purchase and develop, through deployment and maintenance to decommissioning and disposal, the information security of personal information should be considered.

The selection of solutions should embrace the principles of privacy by design and privacy by default, including where encryption is required (see control A.3.26), with systems embracing secure engineering principles including:

- Using multiple security solutions to address specific security issues;

- Considering physical and logical security boundaries;

- Ensuring software development is conducted with security in mind; and

- Performing threat intelligence to inform mitigating controls.

If the organisation outsources any of its development (A.3.30) activities, it needs to ensure these align with its internal practices, embracing the same secure engineering principles to deliver a solution that meets its requirements. Those requirements will need to be agreed contractually (see control A.3.10) and appropriate confidentiality agreements will need to be in place (see control A.3.18).

Finally for the controls considered in this section, the security considerations need to include user endpoint devices (A.3.22) and ensure that personal information processed or accessible via them is appropriately protected.

Test information (A.3.31)

At any stage of process or system development, information used in the testing should use false or synthetic personal information. Where personal information has to be used, the same extent of information security measures should be applied, typically informed by a risk assessment using the same parameters as used to inform control selection in the live environment in the first instance.

CHAPTER 6: CERTIFICATION

As with many other management system standards, there is a scheme that organisations can use to demonstrate their conformity with ISO/IEC 27701.

Organisations wishing to use this scheme to demonstrate the robustness of their privacy information management arrangements need to subject themselves to an external audit.

If the audit and resulting certificate is part of the internationally recognised 'accredited certification scheme', then interested parties will have a good idea of the degree of confidence they can put in the issued certificate. Accredited certificates are issued by audit bodies that are accredited by their local accreditation body. In the UK, this means that the United Kingdom Accreditation Service (UKAS) accredits the audit/certification body. Certificates issued under UKAS accreditation will bear the UKAS management systems accreditation symbol as in Figure 2.

0000

Figure 2: The UKAS accreditation mark

The four-digit number under the UKAS symbol relates to the accreditation schedule that can be viewed on the UKAS website (*www.ukas.com*) and will be used in conjunction with the certification body's logo.

Organisations seeking to demonstrate they conform with the Standard become certified, not accredited.

Accreditation bodies around the world sign up to a memorandum of understanding that results in mutual recognition of one another's schemes – so a certificate issued under accreditation by the ANSI-ASQ National Accreditation Board (ANAB) in the US, the Joint Accreditation System of Australia and New Zealand (JAS-ANZ) or another member of the International Accreditation Forum (IAF[12]) will be the equivalent of one issued under UKAS accreditation – hence a worldwide scheme exists.

To find out if an accredited certificate is the equivalent of those issued under the scheme described here, determine whether the accreditation body is a member of the IAF by visiting *www.iaf.nu*.

The global scheme enables suppliers to demonstrate that they manage information security in accordance with recognised good practice. The confidence this scheme provides means that customers can rely on certification rather than incur the cost of sending their own auditors in to determine the confidence required by their own directors, stakeholders and clients. This can save a lot of time, cost and disruption for both the auditing and audited parties – a benefit that contributes to the uptake of ISO 27701-accredited certification.

It is important to clarify that certification to ISO/IEC 27701 will not be accredited in accordance with ISO/IEC 17065 and hence is not an 'EU GDPR certification' as referenced in Articles 42 and 43 of the Regulation. This is because ISO/IEC 17065 sets

---

[12] The IAF is due to merge with ILAC (the International Laboratory Accreditation Cooperation) to form a single international accreditation organization, Global Accreditation Cooperation Incorporated from January 2026.

out the requirements for organisations certifying products and services. As ISO/IEC 27701 is an ISO management system standard, the appropriate accreditation standard is ISO/IEC 17021, with the accreditation criteria being extended for the PIMS certification scheme by ISO/IEC 27706. Certification to ISO/IEC 27701 will provide an assurance that management processes are in place to protect privacy, with some important caveats as described in this chapter. The assurance that ISO/IEC 27701-accredited certification will provide to the supply chain, enabling clients to lighten the load of supplier audits, is likely to drive interest. Other interested parties that might take confidence from an ISO/IEC 27701-certified organisation include its directors, who will require confidence in their organisation's practices and controls, and consumers.

To achieve certification to ISO/IEC 27701, an organisation will need to submit itself to an audit by an independent certification body (a third party – hence certification audits are often referred to as third-party audits). If those viewing the certificate require a degree of confidence in it, it needs to be an accredited certificate, i.e. a certificate issued by a certification body that has been accredited by an accreditation body. Accreditation is dependent upon a number of controls being in place, including impartiality, competence and appropriate time being spent conducting audits.

A certification audit will involve one or more auditors being assigned by the certification body. Auditors will seek objective evidence to demonstrate conformity with the audit criteria, but it is likely that evidence of nonconformity will be identified. Where this is the case, the auditor is required to document it, grading it as either a major or minor nonconformity – either way, the organisation being audited will have time to address the finding, correcting the issue as well as considering and possibly implementing corrective action. If a nonconformity is major, the certification body will need to validate the correction and effectiveness of corrective action; if the finding is minor, it is possible that the matter can be closed out through correspondence before certification is granted. No matter the grading or how the nonconformity is addressed, the certification body is required to follow up the matter at the subsequent audit to confirm it has been managed in accordance with the requirements of the audit criteria.

The degree of trust that can be put on a certification extends beyond confirming that it is accredited. The scope of the PIMS is stated on the certificate, and this needs to include the business activities that the reader is concerned about – the relevant processing of personal information, and the SoA that identifies the controls that have been determined as necessary along with their implementation status are both directly relevant. Having an accredited certificate of conformity to ISO/IEC 27701, the PIMS scope statement and access to the SoA provide insight as to the level of confidence that can be derived.

Other audit applications

The provision of a specification for a PIMS lends itself to supplier, or second-party, audits. This means that buyers can use the Standard as a recognised and widely available framework against which to conduct supplier audits, knowing that the terms and definitions being used and general approach are set. These can be used to assure themselves that the privacy information management their supplier is providing is in line with the terms of the contract between the two organisations.

Second-party audits can be used to drive continual improvement through the supply chain. However, they can prove expensive and are often only used where the degree of risk warrants them. Often, the assurance of accredited certification, together with some suitably intelligent questioning, is more cost-effective and provides the confidence required.

CHAPTER 7: TERMS AND DEFINITIONS

For general advice that is as applicable to the home as the office, take a look at *www.getsafeonline.org*.

Accreditation: the scheme through which an authoritative body formally recognises a person's or an organisation's competence to carry out specified tasks. Not to be confused with certification. Third-party certification (auditing) bodies become accredited and those they audit, subject to a successful outcome, become certificated.

Certification: the process through which a certification body confirms that a product, process or service conforms to a specific standard or specification. For example, an organisation becomes certificated to ISO 27701:2025.

Certification body: *see* Third-party certification body.

Compliance: a positive answer to the question 'Is what is taking place in line with the specified requirements?' Hence, non-compliance and compliance monitoring. Compliance is often used in a legal context.

Conformance: fulfilment of a requirement. A positive answer to the question 'Is what is taking place in line with the specified requirements?' Hence, non-conformance and conformance monitoring. Conformance is often used in a non-legal context.

Encryption: the conversion of plaintext into code, using a mathematical algorithm, to prevent it being read by a third party.

IEC: International Electrotechnical Commission, a global organization that develops and publishes international standards for electrical, electronic, and related technologies.

ISO: acronym, from the Greek *isos* ('equal to'), adopted by the International Organization for Standardization – the world's largest developer of standards. Its membership comprises the national-standards bodies of countries around the world.

Privacy information management system (PIMS): information security management system that addresses the protection of privacy as potentially affected by the processing of PII (ISO/IEC 27701:2025, Clause 3.3).

PIMS: *see* Privacy information management system.

Policy: overall intention and direction as formally expressed by management.

Risk: effect of uncertainty.

SoA: *see* Statement of Applicability.

Statement of Applicability (SoA): documented statement describing the control objectives and controls that are relevant and applicable to the organisation's PIMS, based on the results and conclusions of the risk assessment and risk treatment processes.

Third-party certification body: independent organisation with the necessary competence and reliability to award certificates following verification of conformance. Organisations should check the accreditation status of such bodies and the schemes they operate before appointing them.

UKAS: United Kingdom Accreditation Service – the sole national accreditation body recognised by the UK government to assess, against internationally agreed standards, organisations that provide certification, testing, inspection and calibration services. See *www.ukas.com*.

FURTHER READING

GRC Solutions is the world's leading publisher for governance and compliance. Our industry-leading pocket guides, books and training resources are written by real-world practitioners and thought leaders. They are used globally by audiences of all levels, from students to C-suite executives.

Our high-quality publications cover all IT governance, risk and compliance frameworks and are available in a range of formats. This ensures our customers can access the information they need in the way they need it.

Other books you may find useful include:

- *ISO 27001/ISO 27002 - A guide to information security management systems* by Alan Calder, *https://www.itgovernance.co.uk/shop/product/iso-27001iso-27002-a-guide-to-information-security-management-systems*

- *IT Governance – An international guide to data security and ISO 27001/ISO 27002,* Eighth edition by Alan Calder and Steve Watkins, *https://www.itgovernance.co.uk/shop/product/it-governance-an-international-guide-to-data-security-and-iso-27001iso-27002-eighth-edition*

- *EU General Data Protection Regulation (GDPR) – An implementation and compliance guide, fourth edition* by the IT Governance Privacy Team, *https://www.itgovernance.co.uk/shop/product/eu-general-data-protection-regulation-gdpr-an-implementation-and-compliance-guide-fourth-edition*

For more information on GRC Solutions and IT Governance™, a GRC Solutions Company as well as branded publishing services, please visit *https://www.itgovernance.co.uk/.*

Branded publishing

Through our branded publishing service, you can customise our publications with your organisation's branding. For more information, please contact *clientservices-uk@grcsolutions.io.*

Related services

GRC Solutions offers a comprehensive range of complementary products and services to help organisations meet their objectives.

For a full range of resources, please visit *www.itgovernance.co.uk.*

Training services

GRC Solutions' training programme is built on our extensive practical experience designing and implementing management systems based on ISO standards, best practice and regulations.

Our courses help attendees develop practical skills and comply with contractual and regulatory requirements. They also support career development via recognised qualifications.

Learn more about our training courses and view the full course catalogue at *www.itgovernance.co.uk/training.*

Professional services and consultancy

We are a leading global consultancy of IT governance, risk management and compliance solutions. We advise organisations around the world on their most critical issues and present cost-saving and risk-reducing solutions based on international best practice and frameworks.

We offer a wide range of delivery methods to suit all budgets, timescales and preferred project approaches.

Further reading

Find out how our consultancy services can help your organisation at *www.itgovernance.co.uk/consulting*.

Industry news

Want to stay up to date with the latest developments and resources in the IT governance and compliance market? Subscribe to our Security Spotlight newsletter and we will send you mobile-friendly emails with fresh news and features about your preferred areas of interest, as well as unmissable offers and free resources to help you successfully start your project: *www.itgovernance.co.uk/security-spotlight-newsletter*.

EU for product safety is Stephen Evans, The Mill Enterprise Hub, Stagreenan, Drogheda, Co. Louth, A92 CD3D, Ireland. (servicecentre@itgovernance.eu)

www.ingramcontent.com/pod-product-compliance
Lightning Source LLC
Chambersburg PA
CBHW042118190326
41519CB00030B/7545